Georgie Bailey

these words that'll linger like ghosts till the day i drop down dead

Salamander Street

PLAYS

First published in 2023 by Salamander Street Ltd., a Wordville imprint. (info@salamanderstreetcom).

these words that'll linger like ghosts till the day i drop down dead © Georgie Bailey, 2023

Cover illustration by Hal Darling.

ISBN: 9781914228896

10 9 8 7 6 5 4 3 2 1

Further copies of this publication can be purchased from
www.salamanderstreet.com

Wordville

these words that'll linger like ghosts till the day i drop down dead was first performed at Pleasance Theatre in London on 13th June 2023. The cast was as follows:

Sam / A	Tessa Wong
Charlie / B	Daniel Crespin
Astronaut	Emmanuel Olusanya
Writer	Georgie Bailey
Director	Lucy Betts
Designer	Hal Darling
Associate Producer	Eve Allin
Production Manager	Chloe Stally-Gibson
Lighting Designer	Cheng Keng
Mental Health Champion	Michaela Hunte

ChewBoy Productions

ChewBoy Productions is a multi-award-wining production house dedicated to supporting and developing early-career artists through innovative multi-disciplinary projects that stick. They were the recipients of the Untapped Award (*Caligari*), and an OFFIE for Company Ensemble (*DJ Bazzer's Year 6 Disco*) in 2022, won the Innovative Play at the LPT Awards 2021 (*TETHERED*) and the Best of Brighton Fringe Award in 2019 (*Euan*). The company also produces high-quality videography work for theatres, creatives and arts organisations. This project (*these words*) marks the company's 16th creative project since 2018.

CAST

Daniel Crespin | Actor *(B / Charlie)*

Theatre credits include: *A Midsummer Night's Dream* (UK Tour), *Romeo & Juliet* (European Tour), *Romeo & Juliet* (Albany Theatre), *Hansel & Gretel* (Insane Root), *Emerge Sessions* (Bush Theatre), *Ulster American* (Linbury Studio), *Macbeth* (UK Tour), *Void* (Rondo Theatre/Edinburgh Festival), *Celestial Ark* (Arcola), *The End of History* (Tristan Bates Theatre), *Scrooge the Musical* (U.K. Tour).

TV Credits Include: *The Outlaws* (BBC/Amazon Studios), *Jutland* (Channel 4). Daniel is also a musician, writer and podcast host. Check out *Starving Artists* wherever you get your podcasts.

Tessa Wong | Actor *(A / Sam)*

Tessa Wong is an actress, who trained at Bristol Old Vic where she received the New Earth Theatre's Constellation Creatives Bursary in 2021. Credits include: *Smothered* (Sky), *Black Mirror* (Netflix), *The Capture* (BBC One) and *Midsomer Murders* (BBC).

Emmanuel Olusanya | Actor *(Astronaut)*

Emmanuel Olusanya trained at LAMDA. His work in theatre includes *Phaedra* at the National Theatre, *Lark Rise to Candleford* and *The Snow Queen* at the Everyman Theatre, *Flashbang* at the Lion & Unicorn Theatre, *The Trumpet and the King* for Terra Nova, and *Elegies for Angels, Punks and Raging Queens* at the King's Head. TV includes *Eastenders*. Audio includes *Iron Anthology: The Door/The Lock*.

Georgie Bailey | Writer

Georgie Bailey is an award-winning playwright, poet and producer. In 2023, he won the Adopt a Playwright Award and has been longlisted for Theatre Uncut, Original Theatre and BOLD Playwright's respective awards for his works. Georgie is an alumnus of Soho, HighTide, Papatango, Oxford Playhouse and the Criterion's respective playwriting attachments and his works have been seen in a variety of places such as Chichester Festival Theatre, Pleasance, New Diorama, Underbelly Edinburgh and BBC Audio Labs.

Lucy Betts | Director

Lucy Betts is an OFFIE 2022 Winning Director (Best Director) and an associate of the Watermill Theatre where she's been involved with four productions since 2019. She's with Hull Truck Theatre, Chichester Festival Theatre, Jermyn Street and a string of drama schools with a focus on actor-musician performance. Lucy is the Resident Director of ChewBoy Productions.

Recent Credits include: *Lone Flyer* (Jermyn Street, Watermill, Hull Truck), *Tipping the Velvet* (GSA), *Sleeping Beauty* and *The Wizard of Oz* (Chichester Festival Theatre), *Caligari* (New Diorama, Edinburgh Fringe), *Groundhog Day*, *The Tempest*, *Nell Gwyn*, *Jekyll and Hyde* (Rose Bruford).

Hal Darling | Designer

Hal Darling is a designer, actor, artist and filmmaker. After completing an art foundation (with distinction) where he focussed on creating visual art, Hal has worked in theatre both behind the scenes and in front of them. Hal has appeared in nine productions with Chichester Festival Theatre in professional and youth roles. In 2018, Hal founded ChewBoy Productions with Georgie Bailey where he is the head of Film, Branding and Design.

Credits include: *these words that'll linger...* (Bitesize Festival, Rehearsed Reading), *Caligari* (New Diorama, Edinburgh Fringe), *DJ Bazzer's Year 6 Disco* (Golden Goose, Riverside Studios), *TETHERED* (Rose Theatre, Lion and Unicorn) and *Euan* (UK Tour).

Eve Allin | Associate Producer

Eve Allin is a freelance producer for theatre and dance. She is lead producer at Broccoli Arts, a producing company making work for/by/about lesbian, bisexual and queer people who experience misogyny. She was recently Associate Producer at Soho Theatre and is the producer for internationally award-winning artists Jaz Woodcock-Stewart, Nathan Ellis and Jennifer Jackson.

Chloe Stally-Gibson | Production Manager

Chloe Stally-Gibson is a freelance lighting designer, production and stage manager. She graduated from Guildhall School of Music & Drama with a BA in Theatre Technology and Mountview with an MA in Creative Producing. Chloe is the Technical Manager of ChewBoy Productions.

Credits include: *Perfect Show for Rachel, Bossy* (ZooCo), *The Secretaries* (Young Vic), *4th Country* (Park Theatre), *Telethon* (Shoreditch Town Hall), *DJ Bazzer's Year 6 Disco* (Golden Goose, Riverside Studios), *Tell Me Straight* (Chiswick Playhouse).

Cheng Keng | Lighting Designer

Designer/Scenographer. Trained at National Taiwan University of Art and Royal Central School of Speech and Drama.

Theatre includes: *The Retreat* (Finborough Theatre), *The Zone* (Taoyuan Art Centre), *A Hundred Words of Snow* (OSO Art Centre), *Pennyroyal* (Finborough Theatre), *Sankofa: Before the Whitewash* (Roundhouse), B*irdie and the Animal Kingdom* (Harrow Arts Centre), *Beauty and the 7 Beasts* (Brixton Jamm), *Borders* (Drayton Arms Theatre), *7homes* (online exhibition), *Extremist* (Royal Central School of Speech and Drama), *Blue Island 99* (International Dublin Gay Theatre Festival and Sydney Fringe Festival) and *Hello World* (NTT, Taiwan).

Michaela Hunte | Mental Health Champion

Michaela Hunte is a trainee psychotherapist and empowerment coach in the arts. Believing that mental health is equally as important as physical health, she aims to create positive change in the way we view mental health and wellbeing. Working as a Mental Health Champion in many different settings, Michaela supports and empowers others as they embark on their healing journey, offering a listening ear and safe space to talk.

these words that'll linger like ghosts till the day i drop down dead

Georgie Bailey

CHARACTERS

A | SAM   Older

B | CHARLIE   Younger

ASTRONAUT   Voiceover

NOTES

The second part of the play is set out in a rehearsed reading format.

Whenever characters are denoted by **A** / **B**, we are in the world of the play, they speak to each other as characters.

Whenever characters are denoted by **SAM** / **CHARLIE**, they're speaking to one another as humans, as actors.

For your production, you may choose to use the actor's own names. You may prefer to use the ones I've provided. Your call, boss!

PROLOGUE

As the audience enters, projected on the wall: THESE WORDS THAT'LL LINGER by Sam Pinney.

There is an astronaut attached to the lighting rig, dangling down. This could also be projected, I don't really mind, whatever fits your bank and style best.

On clearance…

PART A | The Imagined

The sound of static. A blank room.

*An actor, **SAM**, enters. They will play **A**.*

A living, breathing human taking up a shared space.

They face other living, breathing human beings in the audience.

They could be in black clothing. They could not.

They build a Jenga tower. It takes as long as it needs to.

*After a moment, a second actor, **CHARLIE**, takes up the space.*

*They will be playing **B**. The pair take each other in for a moment.*

SAM: Thank you for doing this.

CHARLIE: Whatever helps.

And that's how the play begins.

Bright light. Past. Hospital.

A: What was the last thing you remember?

B: It were bright.

A: And?

B: And then it weren't as bright.

A: You gotta remember more than that.

B: Ain't nothing more to it.

A: You always wanna tell stories, now you got one you don't wanna—

But you don't have to. You don't have to!

Beat.

Just a good job you pulled through.

Ya silly GOOSE!

Laughter track. Mimicking a live studio audience. Or a sitcom. Weird as fuck.

A: We thought you were DEAD!

Laughter track. Applause.

A: It wasn't your fault, you know.

B: I didn't mean to do it.

A: It's ok if you did. It's ok. It's all forgiven.

B: You're good to me.

A: I couldn't be good without you.

B: I won't do it again.

A: It doesn't matter if you do. It's ok.

B: I won't do it again.

A: It's ok.

B: I'm trying to be better.

A: We all are.

Beat.

I'll do anything I can to help.

B: Thanks for visiting.

A: Anything.

B: It's nice to have visitors.

A: That's what I'm here for.

B: It wasn't your fault either.

A: Thanks.

B: It was mine.

A: It wasn't anybody's.

B: Thanks.

A: Thanks.

Beat.

You'll be alright. It'll be ok. It'll all be ok.

Later.

B: I'm craving Chewitts.

A: Weird.

B: They said it'll do that.

A: When was the last time you ate a Chewitt?

B: Nine? Ten, maybe?

A: Do they still sell Chewitts?

B: I haven't eaten one since I was nine.

A: I'll go find some Chewitts.

B: I knew there was a reason I didn't take these before.

A: You haven't been taking them?

B: I fucking hate Chewitts!

A: You don't!

B: You can eat them with the wrappers on, yano?

A: Will you be alright on your own?

B: Did you know that? You can eat them with the wrappers on.

A: Can that be good for you?

B: Can't be bad.

A: Can't be incredible.

Beat.

B: I'm in the best place I could be.

Later.

A: Weird that she's just down the hall from here.

B: I've not said hello.

A: You don't have to.

B: Do you think that's bad? I've not said hello.

A: I think it would be hard for you both, given the...

B: You're right.

A: And anyway, she'd just want you to look after yourself.

B: It's been a long time.

A: Very long time.

B: Sorry, that I wasn't...

A: It's ok. Quite liked wiping her arse after a while. Closer to her.

B: Probably nicer ways to be closer to your Mum.

Beat.

B: Sorry I never wiped her arse.

A: You're glad you didn't, to be honest.

B: Don't go painting pictures.

A: Sweetcorn Saturdays were the worst.

Beat.

She doesn't look great.

B: God.

A: More and more like a turtle each day.

B: A turtle?

A: That's what they said it does, what she's got. Sc-er-lo-doma. Scleroderma.

B: A turtle.

A: Like the shell. That's what her... and her face is ... yeah, turtle like.

B: There's a word for that.

A: Turtle?

B: No, no ... it's like... the shell. There's a word for it.

A: Shell?

B: No.

A: Skin?

B: No!

A: Husk?

B: Carapace.

A: Carapace? Never heard of it.

B: Carapace. Beautiful word, don't ya think?

A canned 'AWWWWH' is heard.

B I don't think I like it here. They said I could leave but... I'm not sure where I'd go. But I know I need to... need to go so...

Beat.

This isn't the right place for me. Would it be ok... um... if...

The crowd go WILD. Cheers. Applause.

Beat.

*Back home. The family home. **A** has lived here a while.*

A: As long as you like.

B: Only for a bit.

A: It doesn't have to be temporary. As long as you like.

B: Don't wanna outstay my welcome.

A: It's nice to have company.

B: To a point.

A: You haven't been here before have you?

B: First time.

7

A: Bigger, since Dad left.

B: Is it, yeah?

A: Sad at the time but...

B: Better now?

A: Happier. That's difficult, isn't it?

B: Death is a complicated thing.

Beat.

A: Carapace, was it?

B: Mm.

A: Like a carapace, this place, now.

Beat.

It's nice to have others around.

B: I'll be like a visitor.

A: You're a guest.

B: I'll be like a bug, one that pays rent.

A: You don't have to pay rent, not yet.

B: I'll be like a ghost, I promise.

Beat.

Won't hear a peep outta me!

A: Don't be like a ghost.

B: Was a joke.

A: I don't like the joke.

B: Sorry.

A: Be a human.

B: I will.

A: Or a bug.

B: I'll choose human.

A: Don't be like a ghost.

Beat.

You stay as long as you like. Will be like when we were kids!

B: Under one roof again!

A: And we can play so many games!

B: Like we used to!

A: Are you excited?

B: I'm SO excited!

A: I'M GLAD

A and B play Jenga for a while. It is playful, childlike.

A: This is much better than the other one.

B: What one?

A: The other game, when Mum couldn't afford—

B: Which game?

A: The word game! It were really boring.

B: Was it the really boring one?

A: All we did was link up words!

B: BORING.

A: DULL.

B: MONOTONOUS.

A: REPETITIVE.

B: CYCLES.

A: RECYCLE.

B: CLIMATE.

A: WORLD SAVING.

B: DOUBLE! RESTART.

A: What?

B: It's coming back to me now. You say two words, you have to restart.

A: That's no fair.

B: And if you say a word someone else said, you have to restart too.

Beat.

But it is SO boring.

A: You always win these games!

The sound of audience applauding.

Beat.

Later. Kitchen Table.

B: And they reckon, right, they reckon, like, have you seen that Tintin episode? I think we watched it, you used to put it on as kids, when I were a kid, when we had the Orion tele? I think? The big box one? Or was it a... and anyway, this Astronaut got sucked away into space, right, got taken right away and that was it. Detached. Off. Into the stratosphere or the... I dunno the technical terms but... got me thinking yano like, did he ever return to Earth?

Or was he just out there? Forever more? No one hearing him?

No one able to contact him? And does he die?

A: And did he die?

B: I dunno if they showed that bit. Or I might've gone out to play.

A: Never seeing things through. It must run in the family!

Laughter track.

CHARLIE: Life was easier back then. Wasn't it?

A: It must run in the FAMILY!

Laughter track. There's an indication something is wrong.

A: We used to have FUN! And we're having SO much NOW!

CHARLIE: Sam?

*SAM signals **CHARLIE** to continue on.*

MEMORY. Childhood. A pop song from the 2010s is playing. Maybe a banger like Replay by Iyaz.

A: Turn that shite off. It's so year seven.

B: I am year seven.

A: You wanna listen to this?

A plays something else.

B: No, I don't.

A: Do.

B: Don't.

A: Do.

B: Don't.

A: Do.

B: Don't.

A: Don't

B: Do.

A: HA!

B: MUUUUUM.

Beat.

PRESENT. Home. The pair are still playing Jenga.

B: Tired.

A: Little longer?

B: Can't.

A: Ok.

Beat.

Tomorrow morning?

Beat.

It'll be nice. Nice long walk. Down by Malley's.

Beat.

Only if you want to, though, of course. Entirely up to you.

Beat.

Tomorrow. Down by Malley's.

B: Scler-o-der-ma? Such an odd name.

A: Hard to say.

B: Is it curable?

A: She'll be alright.

B: Proper fighter.

A: Very brave.

B: Very.

A: That's our...

B: That's her.

A: She'll be alright.

B: She'll be alright.

A: We'll be alright.

B: She'll be alright.

A: Are you alright?

Beat.

It'll all be alright.

Don't you just love the Sea?

Beat.

*Later. **B** holds an envelope.*

A: What's this?

B: Just a bit of... to say thank you.

A: You don't have a...

B: I have some...

A: How?

B: Saved.

A: I can't take it.

B: I need you to take it.

A: I'll take half?

B: You'll take it all.

A: I'll take half or none.

B: Half it is.

A: Does this mean you're... because you don't have to, you-

B: No, it...

Beat.

Just to say thanks.

*IN-BETWEEN. Neither here nor there. We've stepped out of the play. An astronaut. Floating in space. **A** and **B** watch it awhile.*

B: This doesn't feel very real.

A: This is real. Trust me.

B: Come on.

A: Can't we stay a while? Here?

B: I don't know where this is.

A: It's fun to be places you don't know.

B: We can't stay here.

The astronaut remains in place, for now...

Beat.

Present.

CHARLIE: Hold. Just hold on.

SAM: Charlie, we're–

CHARLIE: I just don't think they'll get—

SAM: They'll get the astronaut! They will!

CHARLIE: But we haven't explained—

SAM: That's the point of plays! That's what they always do! They leave you in suspense! Now, please. Can we just...

CHARLIE: But you can't just-

SAM: CAN WE JUST—

SAM indicates towards the audience to tell CHARLIE to continue.

B: No astronaut has ever been lost in space.

A: Do you take milk?

B: Or at least that's what they want you to think.

A: Always forget.

B: Just a splash.

A: Sugar or—

B: Because they wouldn't, would they? They wouldn't tell us if an astronaut had been lost in space, or we'd all panic. We'd all stay up all night worrying, contemplating what it'd be like to be totally, utterly lost in the void. Lost in space. Like that bit in Interstellar, where he pushes the books off the shelf to try send a message, try get help, or the bit in Gravity where Sandra Bullock just gets like fucking blasted into the middle of—

A: Do you want a VIB?

B: A VIB?

A: New fancy digestive. Very Important Biscuit.

Break.

VIB?

B: I'm good, thanks.

A: I think we'd know if an Astronaut was lost in space.

B: How could we ever know?

A Something would be left behind.

B: But how would we know it belonged to them?

A: We just would, ok?

CHARLIE: Alright.

SAM: What?

CHARLIE: I said alright.

SAM: What do you mean by 'alright'?

CHARLIE: Nothing, just, alright.

Break.

SAM: Don't argue with me.

CHARLIE: What?

SAM: That's not fair. Be fair.

CHARLIE: What're you on about?

SAM: We're meant to get along. In this version, in my... we're–

CHARLIE: We are getting along. They are getting along.

SAM: This is how it was supposed to happen. Us getting along.

CHARLIE: This isn't about us.

CHARLIE refocusses.

B: Sorry.

A canned 'AWWWW' is heard.

B: Let's... let's get along.

Break.

Days later.

A: A job might really help.

B: I think you're probably right.

A: I'll get the paper on the way home.

B: I love the paper!

A: It's always such good news!

Break.

Morning of interview.

A: How do you feel about it?

B: I'm quite nervous!

A: It's natural to feel nervous.

B: Do you think the astronaut feels nervous?

A: Probably! We all feel nervous from time to time.

Break.

You've got this in the bag, I think. Try again.

B: I'm a hardworking, dedicated individual with a personable, dedicated, can-do attitude. My previous employers have stated how much of a valuable, dedicated asset I can be to any team, and, as a bonus, I can make a great cup of tea in a very dedicated fashion!

A: Anything else?

B: I'm very dedicated.

A: YOU'VE GOT THE JOB.

B: REALLY?

A: WE'RE PROMOTING YOU.

B: THANK YOU.

A: YOU OWN THE COMPANY NOW.

B: I'M NOT SURE I'M QUALIFIED.

A: DON'T WORRY – NOBODY IS - FOR ANYTHING.

B: AMAZING.

A: PLEASE DON'T LEAVE, EVER!

B: I NEVER WILL!

Break.

A: I think you've got it in the bag.

B: You never know what they want.

A: They'll want you.

B: Can only hope.

A: You got this.

B: I got this.

A: I'll be rooting for you.

Break.

Earlier. A few days before.

B: They called today.

A: Ok.

B: Said she's getting worse.

Break.

Said she might not...

SAM: No, not... we cut...

CHARLIE: Oh.

SAM restarts the segment.

B: They called today.

A: Ok?

B: Said she was doing ok.

They can't be sure what's in store for her, though.

SAM: What? No, that's not what I have down. That's...

SAM whispers the new lines in CHARLIE's ear.

B: They called today.

A: Ok!

B: Said she's doing incredibly well. They think they've found a cure!

A: THEY'VE FOUND THE CURE!

B: SHE WILL GET BETTER!

A: SHE WILL!

B: How does a tortoise live to be so old?

A: They look like death by the time they're–

B: They look so wrinkled.

A: Like crinkle-cut crisps.

B: Does she look like that?

A: She's getting better, they said so!

B: Imagine if they made tortoises into astronauts.

A: A space tortoise.

B: That would be sick.

A: Sick in the head, yeah.

B: How would you get a suit to fit a tortoise?

A: People have done stranger things.

B: Reckon PETA would have somethin' to say about it.

A: Peter who?

B: No, PETA.

A: Yeah, who's Peter?

B: No, for Christ sake it's... you know the animal people.

A: Ohhhhhh, you mean P.E.T.A.

B: I don't think anyone's ever pronounced it like that.

A: I do.

Break.

We're getting along so well.

Break.

Home. The evening after the interview.

B: Gonna go to bed.

A: Ok.

Break.

See you tomorrow. Sure it went better than you thought.

Break.

Sure it was really good. Sure you knocked 'em dead.

Break.

Sure this is the one. I can feel it, that this is the one.

Break.
Sure this is gonna be the game changer. Sure you've got it in the bag.

Break.

Sure I'm sure that I'm sure that I'm sure that I'm sure that.

Break.

It's all gonna be alright.

The next morning.

A: When did they say they'd get back to you?

B: Today.

A: Ok.

Break.

Was reading about tortoises today. So, a tortoise's shell is actually part of its ribcage. It's not an exo-skeleton. Or... or something like that, I think. Must be weird. Having something out there, part of you but not part of you at the same time.

B: Turtles and tortoises aren't the same thing.

Beat.

Afternoon.

A: Anything yet?

B: No.

A: Shall we do something to take your mind off it?

B: No, I'm ok.

A: No worries.

Beat.

Tea? VIB?

B: They don't want me, you can just tell.

A: It's only been a day!

B: They said they'd let me know by now.

A: You checked junk?

B: Of course I've checked junk.

A: Good news is just round the corner!

Beat.

GOOD NEWS IS JUST ROUND THE CORNER!

Beat.

Maybe you should... have you... are you still...

Beat.

They said once a day.

B: They aren't helping right now.

A: They might help some day!

B: Not right now.

A: Gotta play the long game!

B: I don't want to play the long game.

A: Patience is key in these—

B: Everything feels dark, I can't feel anything in my body.
It's like a tunnel, like I'm going through this, this and there's
no—

SAM moves everything on in a whirlwind in some form or another.

B: I GOT THE JOB!

THE CROWD GOES WILD!!!!

A: AMAZING!

B: I CAN'T BELIEVE IT!

THE CROWD GOES EVEN WILDER!!!!

A: I ALWAYS KNEW YOU'D DO IT!

B: I START NEXT MONTH!!

THE CROWD GOES SAFARI!!

A: BACK ON YOUR FEET! BACK ON YOUR FEET!

B: BACK ON MY FEET! BACK ON MY FEET!

A: BACK ON YOUR FEET.

                                      B: BACK ON MY FEET.

A: BACK ON YOUR FEET.

                                      B: BACK ON MY FEET.

A: I ALWAYS KNEW YOU HAD IT IN YOU!

The crowd dies down from their frenzy.

B: I'LL MOVE OUT SOON!

The crowd dies down from their frenzy.

A: YOU DON'T... you don't have to.

B: I'LL BE OUTTA YOUR HAIR IN NO TIME!

A: No rush for that.

B: THE BEST NEWS EVER!

A: THE BEST... The best news ever.

Break.

A few days later.

B: So many... boxes.

A: Always boxes.

B: Never tell if boxes are good or bad things.

A: Depends on how you see them.

B: Depends on where you're going.

Break.

A: Don't leave.

B: I have to.

A: A little longer?

B: Got the boxes out now.

A: They can go away again.

B: You'll be ok.

A: Will you?

The astronaut is illuminated. A can see it. B cannot.

A: When I was a kid.

B: I hate these conversations.

A: Don't hate them right now.

B: I love these conversations.

Break.

When you were a kid?

A: When I was a kid, all I wanted to be was a pilot.
Cus I thought, when things got too hard, I could just fly somewhere.
Cus I thought, when I didn't understand stuff at school, or if the teacher shouted at me, or if they threw water on me in the changing rooms, I could just fly off, piss off, fuck off to some other place I didn't know.
I'd dream about places I'd never even seen, like Timbuktu and the Philippines, Dublin, Amsterdam and the Pyrenees and everywhere in-between. And I think about how we'd go together, me, you, Mum.
We'd take a plane, with me as the captain.
And we'd go someplace faraway.
And we'd see ourselves in all the beautiful places we'd travel to.
Your skin mapped in the Rocky Mountains.
Mum's tears washed away in the Pacific Ocean.

My mind calmed in the Grecian air of Rhodes.
Our lives, together, again,
Wherever we may be.
Wandering, meandering together.
Piecing together our puzzle pieces again, technicolour, no cracks.
And every sun we'd walk towards would always be setting,
In that beautiful place between
The lightness and the dark.

Break.

B: Can you help me pack?

Later.

B: Will they let her out soon?

A: She's getting better! They found the cure!

B: Funny they haven't said anything since, though.

A: She's getting better!

Break.

I think you should stay while you start the job. Ease you in.

B: Really?

A: It's a big step. You don't want to do too much at once.

Break.

How're you feeling about starting?

B: It'll be alright.

A: It's really exciting! I'm really excited for you! It's a brand-new world out there!

Break.

Are you still taking them?

B: I feel sick.

A: Really? Do you take them with food—

B: I never have before.

A: Do from now on.

B: Why do some people need to and some people don't?

A: Everyone has to have them with food.

B: No, I mean—

A: Otherwise they feel sick.

B: It just doesn't seem fair. Some people have to take things like this.

To make things better and some...

A: That's why you gotta eat.

B: How some people draw lucky in life. And some people don't.

A: First world problems aye?

B: What?

SAM: No, go back.

SAM reverses the scene.

A: That's why you gotta eat.

B: How some people draw lucky in life,

And some people don't.

A: You drew lucky!

CHARLIE: No he fucking / didn't

SAM reverses the scene.

A: That's why you gotta eat.

B: How some people draw lucky in life,

And some people don't.

A: Come on, let's do something!

*A tries to play Jenga. Takes their turn. **B** is staring at the astronaut. **A** cannot see it.*

A: Oi.

You alright?

CHARLIE: She's going to die.

SAM: She's not.

CHARLIE: She is.

SAM: Not in this version.

CHARLIE: This isn't how things went. This isn't how they
happened.

You can't / do this

SAM coerces CHARLIE to continue. They signal to the technician.

B gets more involved in Jenga. The two play for a while. The astronaut is gone.

A: Didn't you wanna be an astronaut when you grew up?

B: When I were a kid.

A: What happened to that?

B: I grew up.

A: We all have to dream though.

CHARLIE: Dreaming gets you into sticky situations.

Makes you think things are possible when they ain't.

Later.

A: Do you need me to get you anything?

26

B: Like what?

A: I dunno... do you need like, pencil cases for work?

B: A pencil case?

A: I dunno.

B: Maybe, I dunno.

A: Never know if pencil cases are more for school.

B: Probably.

A: So no pencil case?

B: No. Don't think so.

A: That's ok.

CHARLIE: Sam? Sam.

> *CHARLIE continues on.*

B: I'm scared, I think.

A: That's ok.

> *CHARLIE drops again.*

CHARLIE: I don't think I can do this.

SAM: Don't be so selfish.

CHARLIE: This isn't real. They never went to the theatre.

SAM: We did.

CHARLIE: I don't remember you two ever going.

SAM: Mum took us as kids. Me and him.

CHARLIE: They'd never been on a stage. He never mentioned—

SAM: I know but... but this is fun! Another game?

CHARLIE: They had stage fright.

SAM: Come on now, we're having / fun

CHARLIE: This doesn't feel... right.

> *CHARLIE looks up at the astronaut.*

> *A long silence. SAM looks up at the astronaut. CHARLIE follows suit.*

CHARLIE: I want to go home.

SAM: Word game.

CHARLIE: No.

SAM: Word game.

CHARLIE: Please.

SAM: Thanks.

CHARLIE: Stop.

SAM: Last

CHARLIE: No.

SAM: Repeat! Restart.

CHARLIE: Sense.

SAM: Lost

CHARLIE: Astronaut.

SAM: Space.

CHARLIE: Void.

SAM: Absence.

CHARLIE: Death.

SAM: Unreal.

CHARLIE: Imagined.

SAM: Real.

CHARLIE: She's gone.

SAM: Two words! Restart.

CHARLIE: She's—

SAM: Not in this. No.

CHARLIE: End. Finish.

SAM continues in character, reading.

A: They said she was getting better. We'll be alright. Are you alright? We'll be alright.

Break.

Hey? We'll be alright!

The crowd clap and cheer. Everything is going to be alright.

Break.

Later.

A: We're going away for a few days.

B: Ok.

A: Get packing!

B: What? No.

A: We're going.

B: Work on Monday.

A: Few days.

B: Need to focus.

A: I've booked it for the both of us now.

B: You didn't ask.

A: Nice surprise?

B: Didn't ask for the surprise.

A: It'll be good for us. For you.

Break.

She's going to get better you know. She'll be alright.

Break.

Come away for a bit. Take your mind off things.

B: No.

A: Why?

B: I don't just run away anytime things get hard.

A: I'm sorry.

B: Just go. Have fun. I'll be alright.

Break.

Big day Monday.

A: I'll be back Sunday.

Break.

Don't forget to take them with food!

A leaves for a bit.
They tentatively hover by the exit.
Throughout the next section, they pop their head round the corner, checking in.
B takes some of their tablets. Wanders about. Smiles at the audience maybe.
B stares at the astronaut.

B: How you doing up there?

A voice, distant. Bubbled.

B: What?

Again.

B: I can't...

*Again. **B** just stares. Sits. **A** re-enters. Forgotten something.*
They're speaking, but everything is bubbled.
***B** tries to speak, but everything is bubbled.*
*Everything muffled, horrible. Distant. **A** leaves again in a hurry.*
The sounds of the earlier safari flare up again, muffled, bubbled.
***B** feels as though they're drowning. A ticking clock begins, quickens.*
Suddenly, everything washes over, sound comes back...

Hospital.

B: I'm sorry.

A: It's ok.

B: I ruined your holiday.

A: It wasn't a holiday.

B: Your trip.

A: It wasn't ruined.

B: It isn't fair on you.

A: It doesn't matter.

B: I'm sorry.

A: It's ok.

Break.

A: Mum's just down the hall. They said she's getting / better

***CHARLIE** drops the character.*

CHARLIE: She's not there. She's dying, Sam. Palliative care.

SAM: Woah, alright mate.

CHARLIE: It's true! We can't keep running from—

SAM: She's not.

CHARLIE: Her skin hardened. Her blood is finishing pumping, her heart is stopping. No more oxygen, no more breath left.

A carapace.

SAM: Not in this version.

CHARLIE: In this version, you still haven't even tried to help.
In all your versions, you say different things.
Do different things. Say a word differently.
A new sentence. Play games.
Make food. Offer a tea.
But you never ask. Not really.
In all your versions. You never ask.
You don't wanna talk about it.

SAM: I do care.

CHARLIE: I know you do.

SAM: Don't think I don't.

CHARLIE: I don't.

SAM: It's just hard.

CHARLIE: I know it is.

SAM: It's hard to talk about those things.

CHARLIE: I know it is.

SAM: And it's hard for me to... to accept those things.
Because he was my brother. My own...
And this helps me to...

CHARLIE: Is it? Helping, I mean?

SAM: I do want to talk about them.

CHARLIE: I know you do.

SAM: And I do want to try and help. To try and make things better.

Because I'll always want to make things better.

Break.

So, what can I do to help?

CHARLIE: Do you feel guilty?

SAM: I want to help. We all need help.

CHARLIE: You never asked him that.

SAM begins rebuilding the Jenga block.

CHARLIE: You never asked to help him.

A: Will you play?

CHARLIE: Why're you—

A: I'll win!

B joins in. It's a very happy moment.

CHARLIE: You can't change how these things went.

SAM: It's like they're kids again!

CHARLIE: This isn't.

CHARLIE knocks the tower over.

A: I WIN! I'VE WON! FOR ONCE! I'VE WON!

CHARLIE: It doesn't matter how it went.

SAM: I feel like you aren't celebrating my character's victory.

CHARLIE: Nothing would've changed the outcome.

SAM: This is pretty big, I always / lose

CHARLIE: Stop changing the fucking subject.

Break.

You can't keep doing this.

Break.

Changing everything so that it's ok.

Break.

Nothing would've changed the outcome, ok?

SAM: I can't believe that.

CHARLIE: You have to.

SAM: I can't do that.

CHARLIE: Then let me help you. Let me show you how things really happened.

*He gets out three scripts from his bag, hands one to **SAM**, one to the technician.*

SAM: What's this?

CHARLIE: We'll go through the actual. How it all really played out.
CHARLIE rebuilds the Jenga tower. SAM doesn't help.

*Once finished, **CHARLIE** asks the technician to change the lighting state.*

SAM: I don't want to do this.

CHARLIE: We have to. Because maybe, just maybe... You'll be able to live.

PART B | The Actual

B: Till the day I drop down dead

By Charlie Rayburn

Bright light. Past. Hospital.

A: Why would you do something like that?

B: It's ok.

A: It's not ok.

B: It's not ok to you.

A: It shouldn't be ok to you.

Why would you do something like this? Why would you

punish me? Like this?

B: I'm not trying to hurt you.

A: Well, what are you doing?

B: A points to a plate of food.

SAM: You don't need to specify that, you shouldn't direct the actors.

CHARLIE ignores SAM.

A: And I mean just look at that.

B: It's not that bad.

A: That's a crime.

B: Can't lock a person up for that.

A: Should be able to lock a person up for that.

B: It's just a meatball.

A: Looks more like playdough. Is that what they're doing? Feeding you playdough until you die?

B: I'm not hungry.

A: Is that all they think you're worth?

B: Do you want it?

A: It's disgusting.

Break.

Well, only if you're not going to eat it.

B: Later on.

Does she look ok?

A: Why don't you go see her now?

B: Not up to it. Not sure she'd wanna see me... (*like this*)

A: You're probably right. You know what she gets like.

B: Not really.

A: She doesn't half cry.

B: Really?

A: She looks fine. She's getting better, I think.

B: Really?

A: More than I can say for you.

B: Don't do that.

A: You need to let them take care of you.

B: I don't need taking / care of

A: They're trained professionals, it's what they're here for.

B: I'm not some baby.

A: And yet you won't go see your Mum?

B: Well surely that makes me less of a baby. Not needing my Mum.

Break.

Does her skin still look...

A: Don't.

B: I'm just asking if it's still...

A: Don't do that.

B: I'm not–

A: IT ISN'T FAIR TO DO THAT.

Break.

Leave her alone. It's not her fault she's the way she is.

B: And this isn't mine.

A: See her. Go and see her later.

B: They said–

A: Do as your told.

Break.

B: Later. Hospital.

A: Did you know suicide was illegal until 1961.

B: Imagine that. A corpse in prison.

A: Well, I'm not sure that'd be what'd happen.

B: I'm tired. Do you / mind

A: I don't think they'd put your body in a cage.

B: Maybe they would, before 1961.

A: They wouldn't do that.

B: But how do you know?

A: They just wouldn't.

   Break.

   I think you should move in for a while. Once they let you out.

B: This isn't prison.

A: Once you're better. Mum thinks it's a good idea.

B: I'll be fine.

A: We're not sure if you will.

B: I'll be good.

A: It'll be good for us! Bonding.

   Break.

   Have you got much stuff?

   Break.

   You stay till you're better proper, yeah?

B: (*reading*) B stares up at the Astronaut. Silent. A gap.

A: Mum isn't doing all too good. Said they reckon she might
   only have... have a bit of time left.

   Break.

   I think you need to see her, mate. I think...

   Break.

   Why won't you see her? That's your Mum, mate. Your Mum too.

   Break.

A: Why am I the one putting in all the hours? Doing all the...

Can you fucking LISTEN to me for ONCE in YOUR LIFE!

B snaps away from the astronaut.

B: ...sorry.

A: Where is it you go, when you look out there, away from me? Where do you wish you were? Is it better than here? Is it better than here, with me? Do you like it out there? Would you prefer it out there? Why don't you talk to me like you used to? Why are you different?

SAM takes a moment, before looking up from the script. They shake their head. They don't want to go on. CHARLIE encourages onward.

A: I wish things were how they used to be, before you changed.

Later. Back home. The family home. A begins playing Jenga.

A: You remember this, yeah? This is much better than the other one.

B: What one?

A: The other game, when Mum couldn't afford—

B: Which game?

A: The word game!

B: How did you play it?

A: It was really boring.

B: I think I liked it.

A: No you didn't. We didn't.

Break.

A: We didn't like it. Come on, it'll take your mind off things. Keep you busy.

*A encourages **B** to play. **B** eventually does. **A** begins losing.*

SAM: They want me to lose.

    SAM looks out to the audience.

    You want me to lose, don't you? Fine then.

    SAM topples the Jenga block over.

CHARLIE: They don't want you to lose.

SAM: How do you know? I'm the villain here, I'm the—

CHARLIE: They'll understand. They will, in the end, ok?

B: (*reading*) Later. Kitchen table.

A: Ok, so say for instance there was an Astronaut.

B: There are loads of Astronauts.

A: No, ok, like the one you mentioned.

B: The lost in space one.

A: The one lost in space, yeah. Surely he wouldn't live that long?

B: Why does it have to be a he?

A: Ok, maybe she—

B: Do we have to gender an Astronaut?

A: God sake.

B: What?

A: It's always back to something I've said that's wrong.

B: You've said nothing wrong.

A: You always make me feel like I've said something wrong.

B: You wouldn't feel guilty if you didn't think you'd said
    something wrong.

A: No.

B: Just be careful with your words.

A: Words are meaningless.

B: Words are everything.

A: I think those Astronauts are dead.

B: I think you're wrong.

A: I think they have no hope.

B: I think their life is beautiful.

A: I think you're wrong.

B: I think... I think...

    Beat.

A: Food?

B: Nah.

A: Why?

B: Sick.

A: Boiled?

    Beat.

    Fried?

B: Pollo.

A: Marco.

B: Try.

A: Miss.

B: Fail.

A: Try.

B: Repeat.

A: No.

B: Repeat.

A: Please.

B: Fail.

A: Repeat!

B: Restart.

A: Stay.

B: Go.

A: No.

B: Must.

A: Unfair.

B: Truth.

A: Personal.

B: Personal.

A: Repeat.

B: Truth.

A: Restart.

B: Attempt.

A: Only.

B: Properly.

A: Unfair.

B: Repeat.

A: Different.

B: Next time.

A: Two.

B: Needed.

A: Never again.

B: Two.

A: Needed.

B: Must.

A: Unnecessary.

B: Misunderstanding.

A: Lonely.

B: Wrong.

A: Truth.

B: Please.

A: Unfair.

B: Repeat.

A: Different.

B: Stop now.

A: Two.

B: Unfair.

A: Repeat.

B: Unfair.

A: Repeat.

B: Unfair.

A: Restart.

Beat.

Rent?

B: What?

A: A bit?

B: I just need a bit longer...

A: It's been a while, mate, and I just think, you just need to get back on your feet. No more moping around, think about happy things! Happy places! Think of all the places you could go!

B: Like the Dr Seuss book.

A: What?

B: I'm applying, I am, it's just.

A: I know.

B: I'm just tired, all the time.

A: We're all tired. We all got busy lives.

B: It's not that though.

A: Explain it to me then.

B: It's not that easy.

A: Sure it is.

B: It's not like a tired, tired it's like a...

A: I don't get that. You're either tired or you're not, like–

B: No, like–

A: What? Come on! You can tell me anything!

SAM: I'm always here for you.

CHARLIE shakes his head.

You know that.

CHARLIE gestures to the script.

A: If everyone else can do it, so can you.

Beat.

Stop being so fucking lazy.

Later.

B: And the Astronaut, right, they're caught in the cosmos for the rest of their eternity. And no one can hear them, see? They're speaking, and they're speaking but no one can hear a thing. Just... nothing.

They're visible, they're there in the flesh, but they're just a dot. A speck of light against the inky black well of space. The stars lighting their outline for everyone below to see.

But no one cares once the astronaut has lifted off.

They're just... up there. Away.

Out of sight out of mind.

And maybe, maybe in some ways...

They feel like it was always supposed to be like this.

A has been tidying up the Jenga blocks, not listening to the one thing B's had the courage to talk in-depth about.

A: Why do you always make such a mess?

B: Sorry.

A: I tidied up for your big arrival back home and–

B: Can you... can we... do we have to do this right / now?

A: YES, WE DO.

B: Sam—

A: It was better without you here.

B: Maybe I'll go try again then.

Beat.

And maybe I'll do it properly.

A: See if I care.

B: (*reading*) Later. A flicks through the newspaper.

A: This one looks really good. I think this one would be good for you.

B: I don't have the right skills.

A: You never know what they're looking for.

B: Exactly.

A: I'll write the application for you.

Beat.

B: I'm a hardworking, dedicated individual with a personable, can-do attitude. My previous employers have stated how much of a valuable asset I can be to any team, and, as a bonus, I can make a great cup of tea!

A: How about coffee?

Beat.

B: I'm a hardworking, dedicated individual with a personable, can-do attitude. My previous employers have stated how much of a valuable asset I can be to any team, and, as a bonus, I can make a great cup of tea!

A: Tell us about this gap on your CV.

B I had to take some time away.

A Family issues?

B Personal, well, family, well, both, well, it's always a weird one, well, when people ask about, well, when people try to–

A: And how about your situation now?

Beat.

B: I'm a hardworking, dedicated individual with a personable, can-do attitude. My previous employers have stated how much of a valuable asset I can be to any team, and, as a bonus, I can make a great cup of tea!

A: What about your weaknesses?

Beat.

B: I'm a hardworking, dedicated individual with a personable, can-do attitude. My previous employers have stated how much of a valuable asset I can be to any team, and, as a bonus, I can make a great cup of tea!

A: And tell us about you.

B rebuilds the Jenga set. A distraction. A watches on.

A: Will you talk? Can we talk / about

B throws a Jenga block at A. B completes the Jenga block building. Invites A to play. They play Jenga. B wins.

A: You always win.

B: Maybe you ain't trying hard enough.

(reading) Home. The evening after the interview.

A: How did it go?

Beat.

Rooting for you.

Beat.

This is really exciting stuff!

B: I won't get it.

A: You never know!

B: I don't think I'm ready.

A: No one's ever ready!

Beat.

You have to work hard in life. That's what Mum always used to say.

B: I need a break.

A: We all need a break. That's what the twenty-five days are for.

Beat.

You need to see her.

B: It's hard.

A: It's hard for her.

B: I know.

A: Do you not think it's hard for her?

B: It is, I know it is, it is, it—

A: So don't even compare that. Don't do that again.

Just go and see her.

Beat.

Later.

B: Sorry.

A: Don't.

B: Bad.

A: Ok.

B: Weird.

A: Continue.

B: Feel weird.

A: Restart.

B: No?

A: Double.

B: Bad.

A: Better.

B: Awful.

A: Feeling.

B: Sick.

A: Sick?

B: Sick.

A: Good sick?

B: Bad sick.

A: Right.

B: Headaches.

A: Right.

B: Stomach.

A: Right.

B: Numb.

Beat.

Empty.

Beat.

Not here.

Beat.

Absent.

Beat.

Astronaut.

Beat.

Mute.

Beat.

Lost.

Beat.

Space.

Beat.

Holiday.

Beat.

Break.

Beat.

Tired.

Beat.

Exhausted.

Beat.

Exhausted.

Beat.

Just exhausted.

A: Double, restart.

B: (*reading*) Home. A is reading the paper or is on Twitter.

A: Everyone thinks they've got something these days.

B: Something?

A: And maybe they do, don't get me wrong, maybe they do. But—

B: But maybe they do...

A: They might not.

B: But maybe they do.

Beat.

You only know your own head.

A: When did they say they'd call?

B: Today.

A: Ok.

Beat.

I know it's hard, ok, I do. I know it is. But I'm going through it too.

It's not just you. We have to stay strong. For her. Do you think you can do that? For me? For her?

B: It'll make me... I'll get all... upset.

A: Man up, then.

B: I'll try. Sam? I'll try. I will.

(reading) Later. B arrives home. They are drenched.

B: When did Malley's go?

A: Years ago.

B: Really?

A: It were shit anyway.

B: He used to serve us underage.

A: Exactly.

B: That was good.

A: When we were young. Then you grow up and realise it's a bit...

B: A bit?

A: A bit noncey.

B: Sam!

SAM: Stop using my name in this.

They return to their script.

A: It was. It was a bit noncey. Probably why he closed.

Beat.

Why're you soaking wet?

B: Walking.

Beat.

Was clearing my head. Trying to, anyway. That's how I knew

Malley's was...

I walked into the Sea. Walked as far as I could.
And I thought about Malley and his smile. And his weird laugh.
How he'd be so quiet when you'd first enter, and he'd be

dancing on the tables by the time you left.

I thought about the Astronaut.

Beat.

And I thought about how we wanted to be astronauts when we were kids. About how you wanted to be one first, and then I did cus you were older and I thought you were cooler and then I realised that everyone's really not cool, not cool at all, they're just going through life trying to be cooler than–

Beat.

I didn't get the job.

Beat.

And I don't know what's next for me.

Beat.

And I thought Malley's might have some work, I did.

Beat.

But he's just as washed up on the shore as all of us.

Beat.

And what do we do once we're all dried up?

Beat.

We sink again. Or we drown.

SAM: Or we get out. Get pulled out. Get saved.

CHARLIE: You didn't say that, Sam.

SAM: He didn't say any of this.

CHARLIE: But he wanted to.

B: Or we keep going, back against the tide, for the rest of eternity.

Not knowing where we'll end up, or where we're going.

The scene is reset.

A: Why're your jeans wet?

B: It were raining.

(reading) Later. B builds the Jenga set.

A: No. Don't do that.

B: It helps.

A: Just talk to me without this. Just...

B: *(reading)* B finishes the Jenga set.

Begins playing.

B: Do you find the future as scary as I do?

A: No.

B: *(reading)* A phone rings in the audience. It interrupts the show.
A goes to get it. Picks it up. Talks quietly. Long silence.

A: She's... um.

B: *(reading)* B continues playing.

A: Did you hear me? She's gone.

B: *(reading)* B continues playing.

A: Stop FUCKING PLAYING SHE'S GONE!

B: *(reading)* B continues playing.

A: LISTEN TO ME!

B: *(reading)* A destroys the tower. It is animalistic.

A: WHY DON'T YOU EVER LISTEN TO ME // WHY DON'T
YOU EVER SPEAK // WHY DON'T YOU LET ME KNOW
WHAT'S GOING ON IN THAT FUCKING BRAIN // WHY
DON'T YOU LET ME HELP.

B: (*reading*) The sound of a boxing match bell.

A begins showering more and more words at B.

With every slug of every word, B grows weaker, and weaker, and weaker until they're dizzy, they're spinning and—

SAM: Can you, can you stop? I...

CHARLIE: We're almost finished.

SAM: I don't want to carry...

CHARLIE: We're almost there. I promise.

B: (*reading*) Later.

A: We're going away for a few days. Get packing!

Break.

We're going. Few days. I've booked it for the both of us.

Break.

Nice surprise! It'll be good for us. For you. We can't let this stop us living.

B: She's our Mum.

A: She'd want this. It'll take your mind off things. Come away for a bit.

B: I don't just run away anytime things get hard.

A: Well, you did.

B: What?

A: Well you tried to.

B: You think that's what I—

A: Well what did you do then?

Break.

I've paid a lot of money for us to go away.

B: You should've asked me.

A: I didn't think I had to.

B: And why's that?

A: I'm going.

B: Ok.

A: I'm going.

B: Please don't.

A: Come with then.

B: Don't leave me on my own.

A: You'll be fine.

B: Cancel it.

A: No.

B: I can't be alone.

A: I've paid a lot of money.

B: Sam.

SAM: Stop that.

B: Sam.

SAM: NO.

A: I'll be back Sunday. Don't forget to take them with food.

SAM: I don't understand.

CHARLIE: Listen.

He gestures upward to the Astronaut.

CHARLIE *sets up his phone onstage. He plays a voice-note. As it plays, he fixates on the astronaut. The voice is of Sam's late brother.*

ASTRONAUT: Hey Charlie, mate, um. You alright? Sorry, I know it's been a while, but... and sorry for the... I know it's, um, late and-and all that but... just didn't really know what to, who to, um, and thought... we always talk this shit through so... I dunno I... Sam's gone away for the weekend, or week, or... dunno, think she needs to figure some shit out or... Just a bit, lonely? I think? And... tried to call but assume you're sleeping so just wanted to, just, I dunno, just... I just. I miss how things used to be. Yano? Like I dunno, I miss my family, yano and. And I don't wanna keep feeling like I'm fucking up, like everyone's worrying about me or... I feel like, like that astronaut we were obsessed with. Lost in space. I miss the world, like, how it used to feel, how it felt and... Like I miss Chewitts for fuck sake! How they used to taste before everything tasted like, like, and Furbies, that whole conspiracy around them, were they watching us, recording or like some kinda government device or...
And I miss conspiracy theories! Miss looking up at the moon, or the hologram of the moon, the fake moon and feeling like anything was possible. I miss dreaming, man, I miss wanting, needing. I just wanna be free.
Free like that fucking astronaut and I think about all the words that we never get to say, you know? The words left behind? And they're eating me up, man, they're fucking killing me and—

CHARLIE *stops the recording.*

B: I think about how they'll linger like ghosts till the day I drop down dead.

Beat.

SAM: You're really gonna shoehorn your play title into a voicenote from my dead brother?

CHARLIE: That's not the point, Sam.

SAM: GET OUT. GET OUT AND... and don't, don't come back. You hid that message from me? You... Thank you for all your help, Charlie, but I'm... No. Too much. Too...

CHARLIE: None of it was your fault.

SAM: I can't think that.

CHARLIE: You have to try.

SAM: I'm the older... I was supposed to, to do something, to help to—

CHARLIE: You can think about the words you should've said to make him stay. You can think about the words you shouldn't have. The things you should've done, the things you could've done, the things you would've done, but can't anymore.

We can never see what's going on in another person's brain. No matter how much we think we know them.

Whatever you said or did is never as bad as what you've just read. Remember him for what he was, not what he could've been.

You got this, Sam. You don't need to do this anymore.

SAM: Can you... I need a bit of...

CHARLIE: A bit of? A bit of what, Sam, what do you need to...

Ok. Ok. That's... ok.

CHARLIE exits the space.

PART C | The Residue

SAM is left. They sit with themselves for a long while.

They stare up at the astronaut.

SAM: If only we could all be like you. Why can't we...

Break.

I wish I could understand you.

Break.

And I wish you'd come down here. So we could speak. So this wouldn't all be so...

Break.

So we could be lonely, together.

After a moment:

SAM rebuilds the Jenga set.

Picks up the discarded script. They read it awhile. Look up to the crowd.

SAM hands it to an audience member. All that's written is:

Play Jenga.

Don't apologise.

Don't be embarrassed.

Don't feel guilty.

You're sharing a space with someone.

You're playing a game with someone.

This is one of those fleeting moments in life where someone needs you.

And you don't have to even say a word, if you don't want to.

Don't feel guilty.

The pair play Jenga together.

Halfway through:

SAM: Thank you. This is enough.

The lights shine on the Astronaut a moment, halfway round an orbit.

And then, everything ends the way every play does:

with darkness.